CW01267083

THE WORLD OF WORK

Airport

PHILIP SAUVAIN

Editorial planning
Philip Steele

MACMILLAN

© Macmillan Education Limited 1989
© BLA Publishing Limited 1989

All rights reserved. No reproduction, copy or transmission of this publication may be made without written permission.

No paragraph of this publication may be reproduced, copied or transmitted save with written permission or in accordance with the provisions of the Copyright Act 1956 (as amended), or under the terms of any licence permitting limited copying issued by the Copyright Licensing Agency, 33–4 Alfred Place, London, WC1E 7DP.

Any person who does any unauthorised act in relation to this publication may be liable to criminal prosecution and civil claims for damages.

First published 1989

Published by
MACMILLAN EDUCATION LTD
Houndmills, Basingstoke, Hampshire RG21 2XS
and London
Companies and representatives
throughout the world

Designed and produced by BLA Publishing Limited,
East Grinstead, Sussex, England.

Also in LONDON · HONG KONG · TAIPEI · SINGAPORE · NEW YORK

A Ling Kee Company

Illustrations by Steve Lings/Linden Artists and Sebastian Quigley/Linden Artists
Printed in Hong Kong

British Library Cataloguing in Publication Data

Sauvain, Philip
   Airport. — (The world of work). —
(Macmillan world library).
1. Airports — Juvenile literature
I. Title   II. Steele, Philip   III. Series
387.7'36   HE9797

ISBN 0-333-45970-9

Photographic credits

t = top b = bottom l = left r = right

cover: British Caledonian

4, 5*t*, 5*b* ZEFA; 6*t* BBC Hulton Picture Library; 6*b* Aviation Picture Library; 7 Quadrant Picture Library; 8, 9 ZEFA; 10*t* British Airports Authority; 10*b*, 11 British Caledonian; 14 J. Allan Cash; 15*t* ZEFA; 15*b* Aviation Picture Library; 16*t* British Airports Authority; 16*b* ZEFA; 17 Aviation Picture Library; 18 Chris Fairclough Picture Library; 19*t* ZEFA; 19*b* Barnaby's Picture Library; 20 ZEFA; 21*t* British Airports Authority; 21*b*, 22, 23*t* Aviation Picture Library; 23*b* British Caledonian; 24 Barnaby's Picture Library; 26 British Airports Authority; 27*t*, 27*b* Aviation Picture Library; 28 British Caledonian; 29 British Airports Authority; 30 ZEFA; 31*t* J. Allan Cash; 31*b* ZEFA; 32 British Airports Authority; 33*t* British Caledonian; 33*b* Chris Fairclough Picture Library; 34 ZEFA; 35 J. Allan Cash; 36 ZEFA; 37*t*, 37*b*, 38 Chris Fairclough Picture Library; 39*t*, 39*b* ZEFA; 40 J. Allan Cash; 41*t* British Caledonian; 41*b* Chris Fairclough Picture Library; 42, 43 ZEFA

> **Note to the reader**
> In this book there are some words in the text which are printed in **bold** type. This shows that the word is listed in the glossary on page 46. The glossary gives a brief explanation of words which may be new to you.

Contents

Introduction	4	To the rescue	28
The first airports	6	Air traffic control	30
Around the world	8	Checking the aircraft	32
Who runs an airport?	10	Taking on fuel	34
Inside the airport	12	The flight crew	36
At the terminal	14	On the plane	38
The check-in desk	16	Take-off!	40
Handling baggage	18	Flying cargo	42
Security	20	The future	44
Customs and immigration	22		
Beyond the terminal	24	Glossary	46
The runways	26	Index	48

Introduction

▼ At busy airports with several runways, planes take off and land at the rate of more than one a minute. At these large airports many thousands of people are employed to look after passengers and cargo.

In Alice Springs, Australia, a small plane takes off to pick up a little girl who has broken a leg, and carry her to the nearest hospital. In Topeka, Kansas, a farmer loads his plane with crop-spraying equipment. A plane drops food and medical supplies to the drought victims in Ethiopia. The Schmidt family board a plane at Frankfurt Airport in Germany for their summer holidays in the sun.

People travel by plane all over the world today. Air travel has become one of the most important means of transport. Most people fly in **airliners** to go on holiday, or as part of their work. Airliners are the large planes which are owned and run by companies called **airlines**. Airliners do not only carry passengers. They carry **cargo**, such as newspapers, medicines, mail and machinery as well.

A place to land

All planes need a clear area of land or water on which to land and take off. Small planes can use a short runway, such as a grass field or even a sandy beach. Large airliners, however, need a long runway made with a smooth, hard surface. The airliners carry several hundred people at a time, and many thousands of people are employed by airlines all over the world to look after the passengers and cargo.

Introduction

Working at an airport

In a large international airport, thousands of people work in the offices, workshops, restaurants and shops. They all help to make sure that the airport runs smoothly.

Every day many flights leave for airports in other countries. Flights also go on **domestic flights**, or journeys within the country. All these flights are controlled from a tall building at the centre of the airport called the **control tower**. This is where the **air traffic controllers** work. They organize the movement of the planes in the sky and on the ground.

▼ Airline staff at Frankfurt Airport in Germany meet the passengers as they arrive. They take their luggage and check their tickets.

▼ Keeping the arrivals and departures board correct and up to date is just one of the many jobs to be done by the airport staff.

The first airports

On 17 December 1903 at Kitty Hawk in the United States, Orville Wright took off into the air in Flyer 1. He flew for 12 seconds and travelled a distance of 36.5 metres. Orville and his brother Wilbur were the first people to fly a plane. Their success changed the world. Soon other men and women bravely took to the air.

In 1909, Louis Bleriot flew from France to England. This was the first time anyone had flown from one country to another. Ten years later, pilot John Alcock and Arthur Whitten Brown became the first people to cross the Atlantic Ocean in a plane without stopping. The courage of these pioneers of flight helped to make low cost air travel possible today.

▲ A passenger plane flies over the tea-garden and restaurant at Templehof Airport in Germany in the 1920s. There were very few facilities for the passengers while they waited for their flight.

◄ The job of an airline pilot in the 1930s was very different to that of an airline pilot today. To avoid bad weather over the English Channel, pilots often crossed it no more than 13 metres above the sea!

The first airports

▲ Idlewild Airport in the United States in 1955. With increased air travel in the 1950s, airports began to employ more people and put up better buildings to deal with passengers and cargo.

The first airliners

The early airliners were very different from the huge Boeing 747s, or **jumbo jets**, of today. The early planes of the 1920s carried only 10 to 20 passengers, unlike the jumbo jet which can carry between 350 and 500 passengers. From the 1920s, airliners often carried letters and parcels as well as passengers. This system became known as **airmail**.

In those days, flying was risky. The flights were bumpy because of the weather at lower levels and the passengers were often airsick. The runways were much shorter than those of today, and take-offs and landings were often dangerous.

The pilots of the early airliners not only had to fly the planes, but also had to load the baggage and often had to repair the planes as well. On flights from London to Paris, the pilots carried chewing gum in case it was needed to stop leaks!

The first airliners had few comforts. There were no stewards or stewardesses to serve meals or drinks. The journeys were long, slow and cold. The pilots also had to land frequently to refuel.

Early airports

As the first airliners were small and carried few passengers, they were also costly to run. Yet despite the high cost of air travel there were few comforts for the passengers. Airports were very simple. Many were just fields where the passengers waited in wooden buildings or even in tents. Only a few airports had buildings made of brick or concrete.

The age of flight

By the 1950s, air travel was becoming popular. In 1945, jet engines came into use, and the first jet airliner appeared in 1949. This meant that air travel was faster. When the jumbo jet was introduced in 1969, air travel became cheaper because so many more people could be carried on one flight. This growth in air travel meant that more people were needed to work for the airlines all over the world.

Around the world

Today, there are airports all over the world and in all kinds of places. Some are in remote areas, like the airport at Lhasa in Tibet which is 4363 metres up in the Himalayan mountains. Some airports, such as the one on the Pacific island of Tonga, are so tiny that very good navigation is needed to find them.

Other airports cover vast areas, like King Khalid International Airport at Riyadh in Saudi Arabia, which is the largest airport in the world. However, the world's busiest airport is Chicago's O'Hare International Airport in the United States. Many of the passengers who land at O'Hare fly on to other parts of the United States using domestic flights. Nearly 55 million passengers travel in and out of this airport a year, and there is a take-off and a landing every 39.66 seconds.

Where are airports sited?

Airports have to be easy to travel to from nearby towns and cities. Also, fast, efficient transport is needed to take passengers and cargo on to their final destination after they have landed. However, building an airport in or near a city can cause problems. The noise of jet airliners taking off and landing can disturb people who live nearby. Sometimes the pilots have difficulty landing because of tall buildings. For example, landing in Hong Kong can cause problems because of the skyscrapers. As a result, many airports are built some distance from the cities that they serve.

▼ A remote airport in the Hadramaut region of the People's Democratic Republic of Yemen. In this mountainous, desert region where travel is difficult, the plane can bring in much needed goods.

Around the world

Flying worldwide

There is no other means of transport that needs as much international agreement as air travel. There is no one authority that is in charge of the way that all airports and airlines are run. However, there is great cooperation between the various people involved. Government representatives and airline officials from all over the world meet regularly. They agree on international safety measures, which airlines can fly where and on which routes, and also the fares the airlines should charge. They also enter into agreements about which countries' planes can enter the **airspace**, or the sky, above a particular country.

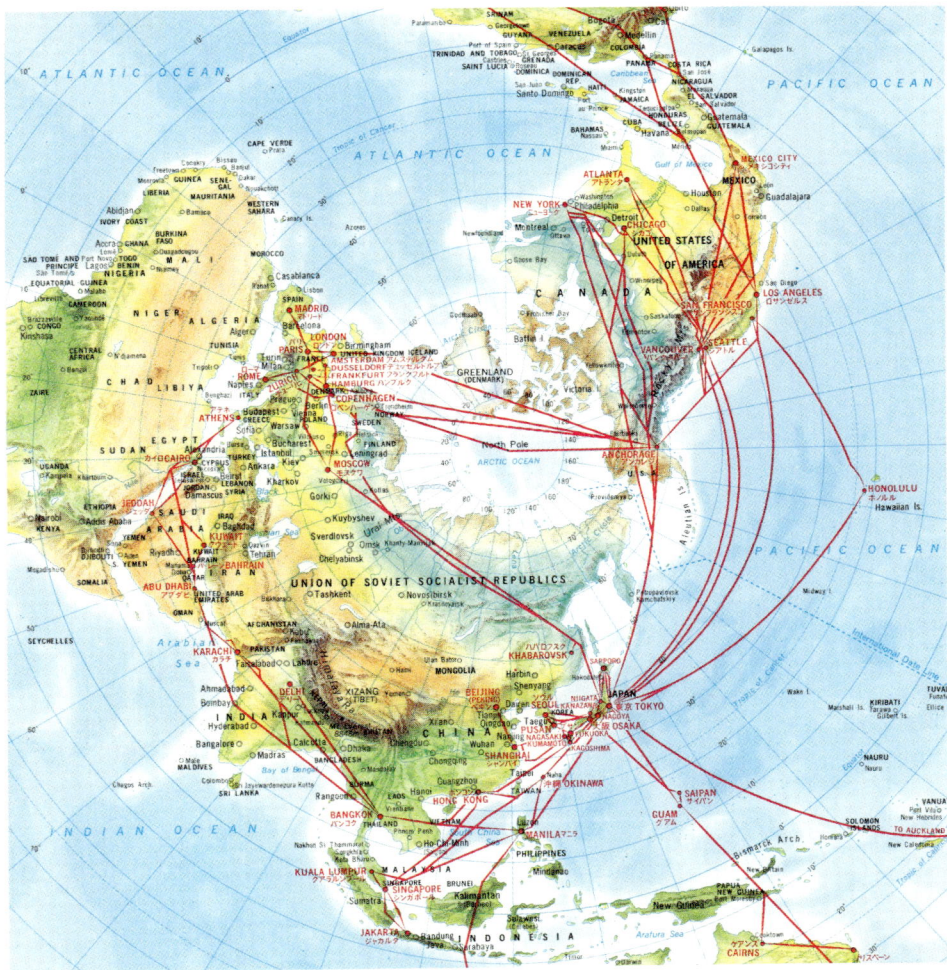

▲ The airport staff at Chicago's O'Hare Airport are kept busy making sure every plane is ready for take-off.

▶ This map shows the journeys flown every month by the airliners of Japan Airlines. A similar map showing all the routes flown by all the world's airlines would look like a spider's web. The thickest part of the web would be over the United States.

Who runs an airport?

▼ The people who run large airports have to plan for the future when more people will travel and more planes will be needed. There are new terminals and runways being built in most international airports.

A large international airport is run by an **airport authority**. This authority either owns the airport or runs it on behalf of a government or a private firm. The airport authority employs thousands of people.

The airport management

The manager, or **administrator**, in charge of an airport has a vital job. He or she has to make sure that everything works smoothly. An administrator is responsible for the choice of the airlines that use the airport. He or she has to act as the link between those airlines or anyone wishing to use the airport's facilities and the airport employees.

◀ Computers can be used by the staff at busy airports to book tickets, plan flights and pay wages.

Who runs an airport?

In larger airports, there may be several **terminal** buildings, and each one has its own manager. These managers look after the day-to-day working of the terminals. There are many problems that arise when a lot of people doing different jobs work in the same building. The terminal managers talk to the people who run the shops, banks and restaurants in the airport.

The airport and terminal managers have to make sure that the airport's police, fire and medical services can deal quickly with any emergency. There may be a fire. An airliner may lose a wheel and have to be towed off the runway. If there is a major accident, such as an air crash, the managers coordinate the airport's emergency services with any that may be needed from nearby towns or cities.

Airport staff

Over 100 000 people pass through a large international airport in the course of a day. The airport staff have to be able to deal with such large numbers. They have to be trained to do their jobs sometimes in difficult conditions. Air traffic controllers may have to deal with hundreds of extra flights during busy holiday times, or after heavy snow or fog.

▼ The flight operations manager has to keep an up to date record of each airliner's movements.

Inside the airport

In large airports, the terminals are either separated into departures and arrivals, or between the various airlines. Sometimes they are divided up according to areas of the world. Whatever way the terminals are used, they are the scene of constant activity.

The administrator's office is usually in the terminal building so he or she can deal with any problems that might arise.

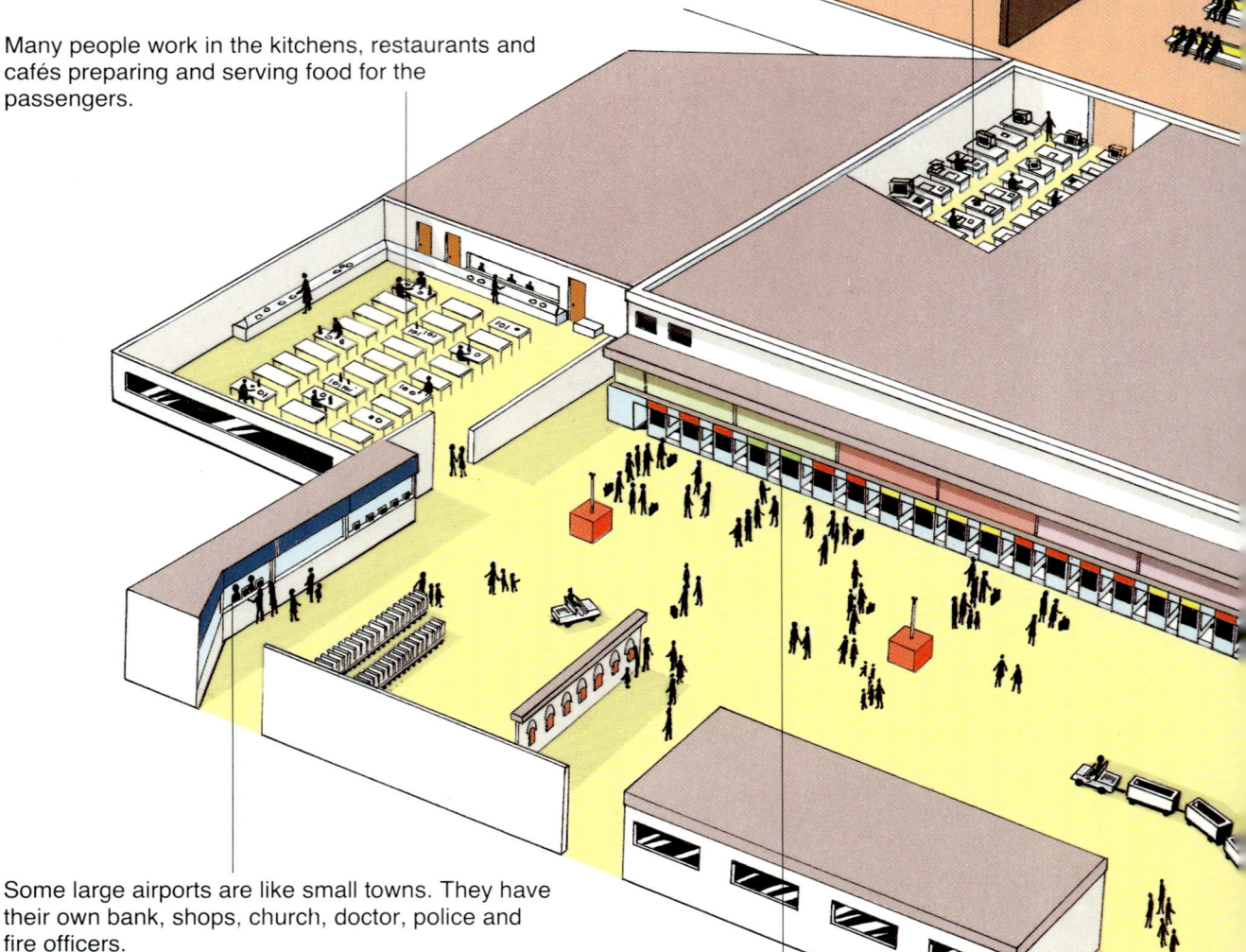

Many people work in the kitchens, restaurants and cafés preparing and serving food for the passengers.

Some large airports are like small towns. They have their own bank, shops, church, doctor, police and fire officers.

At the **check-in** desks, airline staff check passengers' tickets and weigh their baggage.

Inside the airport

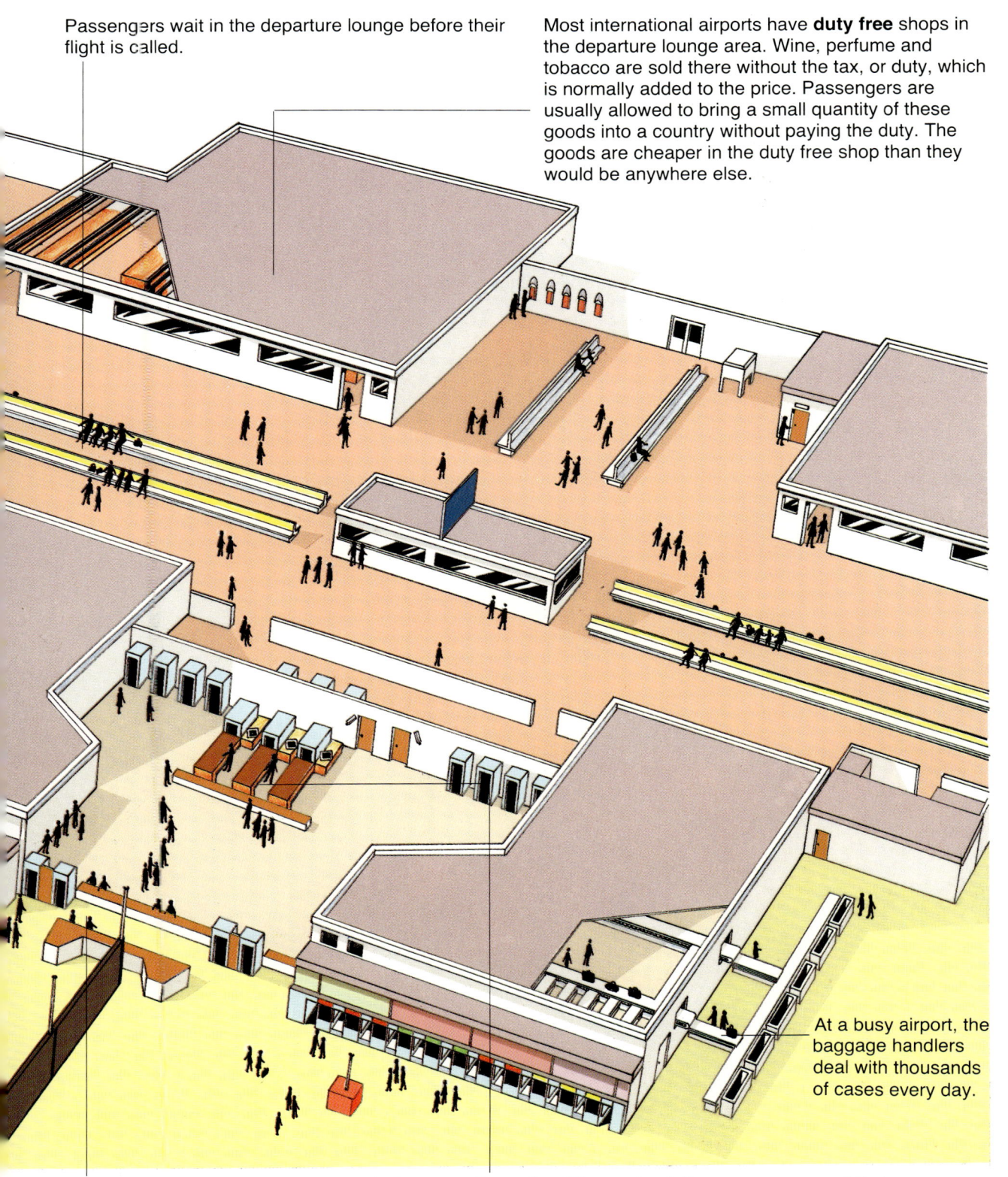

Passengers wait in the departure lounge before their flight is called.

Most international airports have **duty free** shops in the departure lounge area. Wine, perfume and tobacco are sold there without the tax, or duty, which is normally added to the price. Passengers are usually allowed to bring a small quantity of these goods into a country without paying the duty. The goods are cheaper in the duty free shop than they would be anywhere else.

At a busy airport, the baggage handlers deal with thousands of cases every day.

As passengers pass through **customs**, their passports are checked by the customs officers.

Security officers check the passengers and their hand baggage for dangerous objects. Their job is to protect the passengers and airline staff.

At the terminal

The busiest part of the airport is the terminal building. This is filled with the hustle and bustle of travellers, and their friends and families coming and going. Hundreds of workers are employed in the terminal building to serve the needs of the passengers.

Transport workers

The work of an airport begins outside the terminal building. Hundreds of transport workers supply a service to passengers who use the airport. At a large airport, these passengers may arrive at the terminal by train, coach, on the underground or in taxis.

Most large airports have short-term car parks. However, if passengers are going away for several days or longer, some airports have long-term car parks. Some airports employ car park attendants who collect the parking fees. However at many large airports, machines are used to issue parking tickets or the money is collected in the terminal.

▼ Passengers use all forms of tranport to get to an airport. They must arrive at the terminal in plenty of time to catch their flight. Most airlines suggest that the passengers should check in at least one hour before take-off.

At the terminal

Shop assistants

Inside the main hall and the departure lounge of the terminal building, there are shops that sell items like books or make-up that travellers may have forgotten or may need on the journey. Some people also work in shops that sell souvenirs or clothes that people may need while they are away.

Other workers

The terminal also houses many other services for the passengers. Large airports will have cleaners, electricians and plumbers to keep the airport clean, tidy and in good working order. There is often a medical centre with nurses and an airport doctor. Many airports have their own police forces too.

Restaurants and bars also provide jobs for cooks, waiters, waitresses and bartenders.

▲ Passengers change their own money into the currency of the country to which they are flying at the airport bank.

▶ Many staff are employed by airports to work in restaurants and cafés.

The check-in desk

▼ Airports employ information officers to help passengers with any problems they may have. These officers often speak several languages.

When passengers arrive at the terminal building, they go first to the check-in desk. There, the staff of the airline they are travelling with will check their tickets and baggage, and then tell the passengers where they should go next.

Most passengers buy their tickets in advance at a travel agent's or from the airline itself. Some passengers arrive at the terminal without tickets, hoping that there will be some room left on a flight. This usually means that they can buy their tickets at a lower price.

On some flights, it is not possible to book in advance. These are called **shuttle flights**. They are either domestic flights or short-distance flights, and the passengers pay for their tickets when they are on the plane.

▲ Each airline has its own check-in desks and staff. Passengers present their tickets and check in their baggage.

The check-in desk

▶ Every passenger must hand a boarding pass to the stewardess before they can board the plane.

The check-in staff

The check-in staff are always dressed in the uniform of the airline for which they work. They need to be well-organized and patient. They may be faced with a long line of passengers, and with people who do not speak the local language. Some check-in staff are trained in the use of computers which help them to do their job faster and more efficiently. It is possible for a member of staff to deal with as many as 100 passengers in an hour.

Checking the ticket

At the check-in desk, the passenger hands over his or her ticket. The check-in staff feed the details into the airline's computer, or they check them against a list of reservations that is kept at the desk.

If the ticket is in order, each item of the passenger's baggage is weighed on scales and the total weight written on the ticket by the check-in staff. As only a certain weight can be carried by the plane, each passenger is allowed only a limited weight of baggage.

When it has been weighed, the check-in staff put a label on to the baggage which shows the number of the flight and where it is going. The luggage is then put on a **conveyor belt** and sent to the sorting room so it can be put on the right plane.

The passenger keeps hand luggage, such as a handbag and a briefcase. Finally, the check-in staff give the passenger a piece of paper called a **boarding pass** which shows that the passenger has been cleared to board the plane.

17

Handling baggage

Both the airport company and the airline employ a large number of baggage handlers to move baggage between the terminal and the planes and to load and unload the planes. In most large airliners, the baggage is stored in the **cargo hold** which runs under the passenger cabin.

Baggage labels

Busy airports handle as many as 10 000 items of baggage in an hour. When the baggage reaches the sorting room, the baggage handlers look at the labels which tell them where the baggage is going. A flight number such as AA 123 tells them the name of the airline, which is American Airlines, and that the number of the flight is 123. Three other letters on the label give the name of the airport to which it is going. For example, LHR means London Heathrow and MEL means Melbourne.

The sorting room

In the sorting room, a clerk checks the label and puts the baggage on to another conveyor belt. When the sorting clerk presses a button, a machine tips the baggage off the conveyor belt into the right chute for that flight.

▼ Although much of the work of an airport can be done efficiently by machines and computers, it is difficult to handle baggage in the same way. Here, in the baggage sorting-room, the handlers make sure that each passenger's baggage will be loaded onto the right plane.

Handling baggage

Loading up

Baggage handlers pile the luggage for each airliner on to a small **baggage train**. A driver on a small tractor pulls the long line of these wagons on to the area in front of the terminal, called the **apron**, where the plane is waiting. Fork-lift trucks are often used to lift the baggage and load it into the cargo hold of the airliner.

Collecting baggage

When the plane arrives at its destination, the baggage is unloaded. Baggage handlers transport it into the terminal where it is unloaded and put on to turntables called **carousels**. As the carousels go around, the passengers remove their baggage as it appears.

▲ At large airports, handlers use conveyor belts to load the baggage into the hold of the airliner.

▶ Baggage is unloaded onto the carousel and it goes around and around until passengers remove it.

Security

Airlines and airport authorities across the world try to stop passengers carrying guns, explosives and other dangerous weapons on to a plane. This is to prevent anyone from hijacking, or taking over, the plane. Also, if a gun went off by accident, it might kill someone or cause the plane to crash.

Security officers are employed at the airport to protect the passengers and airline staff. It is their job to search all passengers and their baggage as well as to inspect goods being sent by airmail.

Training

The security officers have to understand the way in which weapons or explosives work. If they find anything, they have to know how to handle it safely.

The officers are trained to recognize suspicious behaviour. They must be alert at all times and know everything that is happening at their airport. They must also be in touch with security officers at other airports. To do this, the security officers are trained to use computers. The security officers are helped by reports about suspects sent in by the police.

▼ A security officer watches while passengers pass through the airport's metal detector.

Security

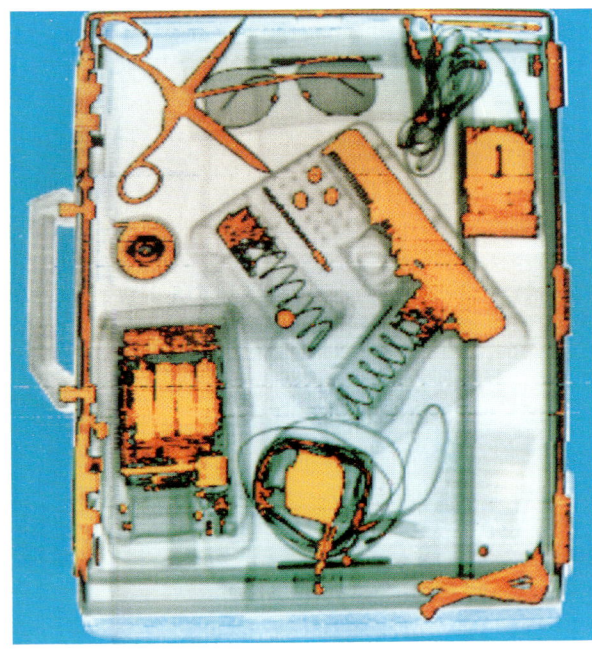

Checking hand baggage

Metal objects, such as guns, can be picked out by the security officers in two ways. First, they search the passenger's hand baggage using an **X-ray machine**. This takes a picture with light rays that show what is inside someone's case. The shape of a gun or knife will show up on the screen even if it is hidden among clothes. Secondly, the passengers have to walk through a **metal detector**. This gives out an alarm signal if there is any suspicious metal object in the passengers' clothes. Sometimes the metal detector is set off by keys, jewellery or belt buckles. Then, the passenger has to remove the item and go through the machine again. If the machine continues to sound an alarm, the security officer will search the passenger.

▲ Security officers pay particular attention to regular flights to countries whose airliners have been attacked by terrorists in the past. Passengers could hide a gun or a knife in their luggage. Can you see the gun in this X-ray photograph?

▶ The luggage is put through a special X-ray machine on a conveyor belt. The officer examines the X-ray image for any dangerous objects.

Customs and immigration

Whenever you visit a foreign country, you must carry a **passport**. This document contains your photograph and gives your name, country, place and date of birth, height and any distinguishing marks. These details are checked by customs officers at the airport. They are trained to make sure that the photograph and details in your passport match your appearance.

Customs officers also check the passports of people returning from a foreign country. This is called **immigration control**. Some passengers may have to carry a special entry form called a **visa**. This allows them to stay in a country only for a given length of time.

If a customs officer suspects a passenger, he or she can feed the passport number into a computer. This will check the number to see if the passport is stolen or belongs to someone wanted by the police.

Baggage check

Customs officers also check whether passengers are carrying dangerous drugs or trying to smuggle in goods without paying customs duties. The passengers are watched closely by the officers. Their baggage may be searched if they look nervous or seem to have something to hide.

Sometimes, customs officers are warned that someone will be trying to **smuggle** illegal goods, especially drugs, into the country. Then they can use specially trained sniffer dogs to help them. Drugs have even been found concealed inside coconuts and chocolates!

▼ Passengers have to pass through passport control before going through customs. The officer at passport control checks the expiry date, the photograph and details in the passport.

Customs and immigration

Preventing the spread of disease

Many customs officers also keep a lookout for people trying to smuggle animals, plants or vegetables into a country. Disease can be brought into a country by infected animals or plants that would infect other animals and people.

Some countries, like Britain, have strict controls on the import of animals. All animals coming into the country have to be kept in **quarantine**. This means they are kept in isolation for a period of time until they are shown to be free of disease. The United States has rules that govern the movement of fruit and vegetables from one state to another. Many large airports have **health control** officers. Their job is to look out for passengers who may be suffering from infectious diseases.

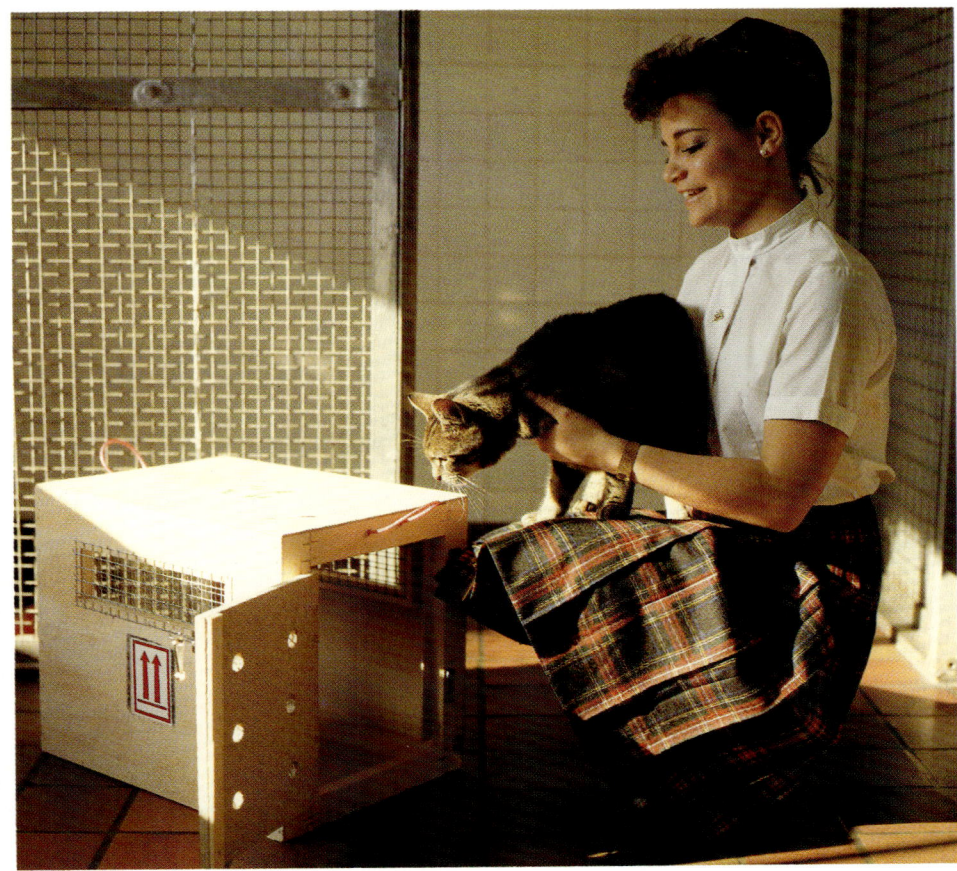

▲ Customs officers test the bottom, top and sides of a bag. Smugglers often conceal drugs or valuables under the lining or in a false bottom.

▶ Animals have to travel in special containers in the hold of an airliner. This is for their safety as well as for the safety of the passengers. When animals arrive in some countries they have to be kept in quarantine before their owners can collect them.

Beyond the terminal

After showing their passports and going through the security checks, passengers wait in the departure lounge for their flight to be called. In many airports, information about flights and flight delays is displayed on a large computer operated board, and sometimes on television screens around the departure area as well. At other airports, regular announcements are made on the loudspeaker system.

▲ The general public is never allowed on to runways at airports. Passengers may only cross the apron when it is time for them to board a plane.

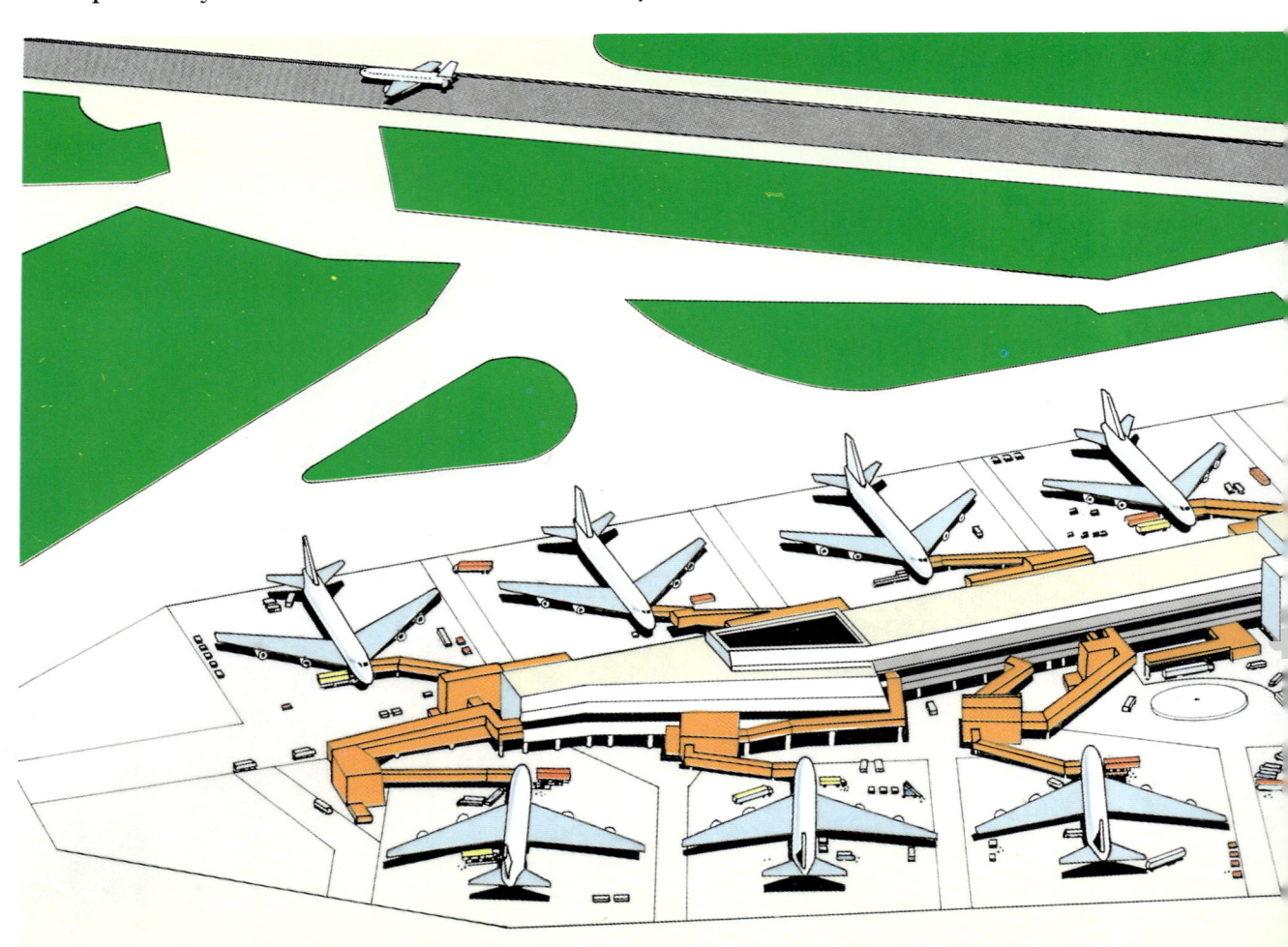

Beyond the terminal

When the flight is called, passengers go to a numbered exit, or **gate**, and show their boarding passes. They walk along long corridors, or **piers**, that lead to the plane. Sometimes passengers are taken by bus across the apron to the plane, or simply walk across the apron and up the plane steps.

Working on the apron

In large airports, the piers which stretch out from the terminal make it possible for several planes to use the terminal at the same time. It is while the planes wait on the apron that engineers, fuel tanker drivers and other workers prepare the planes before a flight. The apron is connected to the runways by a number of concrete roads called **taxiways**.

Permission to use these taxiways and the runways can only be given by the controllers in the control tower, which is usually close to the terminal building. Beyond the runways, there is a **fuel depot** where the tanker drivers fill up their vehicles with fuel for the waiting airliners.

▼ Thousands of airport employees work on the apron or runways at a major international airport. The employees have to carry special security passes.

The runways

Large airports usually have at least two runways. These used to be built so that a pilot could expect to fly into the wind on take-off. The wind helped to lift up the wings of the plane. Today, airliners are so powerful that this is no longer important. Instead, airport officials plan the runways so that planes can land and take off from the airport in safety. Ideally, they do this over the sea or over land where there are very few buildings.

Keeping the runways clear

The engineers who design and build the runways make sure that the surface is smooth and safe for take-off and landing. They, and the airport workers who maintain the runways, are trained to look for weaknesses and cracks. These are repaired quickly when they are found so that the operation of the airport will not be interrupted.

▼ Runways at large airports usually run parallel to one another to avoid accidents. In this photograph taken from the air you can see the two runways above and below the terminal buildings. The diagonal lines that criss-cross the airport are taxiways.

The runways

Maintenance staff sweep the runways clean of stones that could burst an airliner's tyres. In winter, they use machines to blow away the snow. They also use snowploughs to clear thicker drifts. In desert airports, they have to sweep away the sand.

Birds are another problem. They like to gather in flocks at or near airports. This is dangerous for the birds as well as people on the planes because the birds fly into the jet engines. The maintenance staff often use machines which make loud banging or wailing noises to scare the birds away.

Guiding lights

Runways have to be marked out so that they can be seen clearly from the air, especially at night. This is why there are rows of lights on the airport approaches and on either sides of the runways. These lights can be seen by the pilot long before the plane touches down. Electrical engineers make sure that the runway lighting system is working properly and replace any broken lights.

▲ Airport staff use a special vehicle to blow snow or sand off the runways so that the planes can take off.

▼ This car is towing a meter which measures how well it is possible for aircraft to brake on the runway.

To the rescue

The people working at an airport know that one day they may have to deal with an emergency. An airliner may crash. It may catch fire. A pilot may have to make an emergency landing. People may be injured or taken ill on board an incoming plane.

Medical help

Most large airports have a medical centre with nurses, and usually an airport doctor. The staff are always prepared for an emergency. Their vehicles and safety equipment is kept in good working order. They are always in radio contact with the control tower, and are alerted at once if they are needed. In a major crisis, the local police, fire officers and hospitals will also be called on for help.

▼ If the airline knows that someone will be needing medical help, they inform the medical centre. A doctor and nurses can be waiting to help the patient as soon as the plane lands.

To the rescue

▲ Fire officers often use the shell of an old aircraft for practice. Most of the work done by the officers is training for the time when they are needed to put out a real fire.

The fire officers

Most international airports have their own fire officers and equipment. This equipment has to be made to suit the needs of an airport. The fire engines have very long ladders because they have to be able to reach the tail of a jumbo jet which is over 21 metres high. The fire officers aim to be at the scene of a fire within a minute or two after the alarm is given. They expect to put out a fire in less than a minute. They use **chemical foam** instead of water. The foam smothers the burning fuel and stops air feeding the flames. Fire officers know the risk they run if the fire spreads or if the fuel tanks blow up because of the heat of the fire.

The fire officers are also prepared to deal with other dangers as well. Some fire officers have **protective clothing** so that they can enter the burning airliner to rescue passengers. They also use breathing apparatus so that they can breathe in a smoke-filled cabin.

The safety record

Air travel is safe. Crashes are rare. Many airports have never had to deal with a major accident even though thousands of flights leave the airport every year. When a crash or accident does occur, it is very carefully investigated to make sure that the same thing cannot happen again.

Air traffic control

Air traffic controllers have very responsible jobs. They have to control the movements of all the aircraft that are in their area at the same time. Controllers use their skills to help pilots land planes safely in all conditions, in good or bad weather, or in the dark. Controllers have to be alert at all times and think and act quickly when necessary.

Radio contact

Air traffic controllers use radio to keep in touch with planes as they approach or leave an airport. They keep in close contact with the pilots at all times during landing or take-off.

Ground controllers are responsible for the planes as soon as they are on the ground. They make sure that planes do not get in each other's way as they move along the taxiways and runways. The movements of planes on the ground are often shown in the control tower as lights on a huge map of the airport. The ground controllers use this map when telling pilots which taxiways to use. Only the ground controllers can give the pilots permission to take off.

When an aircraft is in the air, other controllers take over. These controllers use **radar** to pinpoint a plane's exact position. Radio waves are sent out, and when they meet the plane, they bounce back and show up on the radar screen as a small blob of light.

Each airliner is fitted with a **transponder**. This is a machine which sends details about the plane to the radar system. A computer which is part of the system changes the information into a code. This is shown on the screen. For example, if the code is BA 123 16 LL, this tells the air traffic controller the position of **B**ritish **A**irways Flight **123**. It also shows that the aircraft is flying at a height of **16** 000 metres. The pilot is flying the plane to London. **LL** being the code for London.

◀ The control tower is always centrally placed so that the controllers have a good view across the entire airport.

Air traffic control

▼ Permission for take-off and landing is given by staff in the control tower. At a busy airport they could be dealing with hundreds of flights an hour.

Controlled landings

When a plane approaches the airport, the pilot radios **approach control** for permission to land. If there are many planes waiting to land, the airliner will have to join the **stack**. This is a system where each plane flies around and around in a circle 914 metres above and below the other airliners in the stack. As soon as the plane at the bottom lands, the pilots in the other planes in the stack drop down to take the place of the plane below. As each plane approaches the runway, the air traffic controllers help to guide the pilots until they have made a safe landing.

▼ The air traffic controllers have to guide all the aircraft on their screen safely on their way.

Checking the aircraft

Engineers do some of the most important jobs at an airport. They make sure that the planes are safe to fly. They check the engines regularly, and make sure that every working part is in order. The engineers can take the plane apart, repair it and put it back together again in perfect working order. They know how to do these jobs well because they are usually trained to do them by the makers of the aircraft.

Service and maintenance

Before a plane flies, it is given a **visual inspection** by the engineers. They look at it carefully to see if there are any obvious faults. They have been given any information about faults that the previous pilot had noted. The engineers check that all the plane's instruments work and are accurate. They need to make sure the plane is safe to fly, or **airworthy**. They also check the tyres.

▼ Many of the routine repair and cleaning jobs on an airliner can be done while it is standing on the apron.

Checking the aircraft

▶ X-ray machines are used to check whether there are any cracks in the metal of the plane.

▼ These engineers are servicing an airliner in the hanger. They strip down the engines and replace any parts that are broken or worn out.

A careful record is kept of the number of hours flown by each plane. After 1000 hours' flying time, the engineers take the plane into a **hangar** for a one-day service. A hanger is a huge garage for planes. The engineers check the plane's engines, tyres, brakes, lights and instruments.

After several thousand hours' flying time, the engineers do a complete **overhaul** on the plane. They examine the metal frame of the airliner closely with X-ray machines. They check to see if there are any cracks. They take out the instruments from the flight deck and test each one. New instruments are put in if there is any sign of wear.

The engineers take the engines apart in order to test the different parts and replace any that are faulty. Each engine is tested until it is working perfectly. Every part of the plane is tested and repaired or replaced in the same way. On some airlines, even the seats inside the passenger cabin are replaced.

33

Taking on fuel

▼ The flight engineer has to keep a constant check on the amount of fuel remaining during a flight. He has to make sure that there is enough to get the plane to its destination.

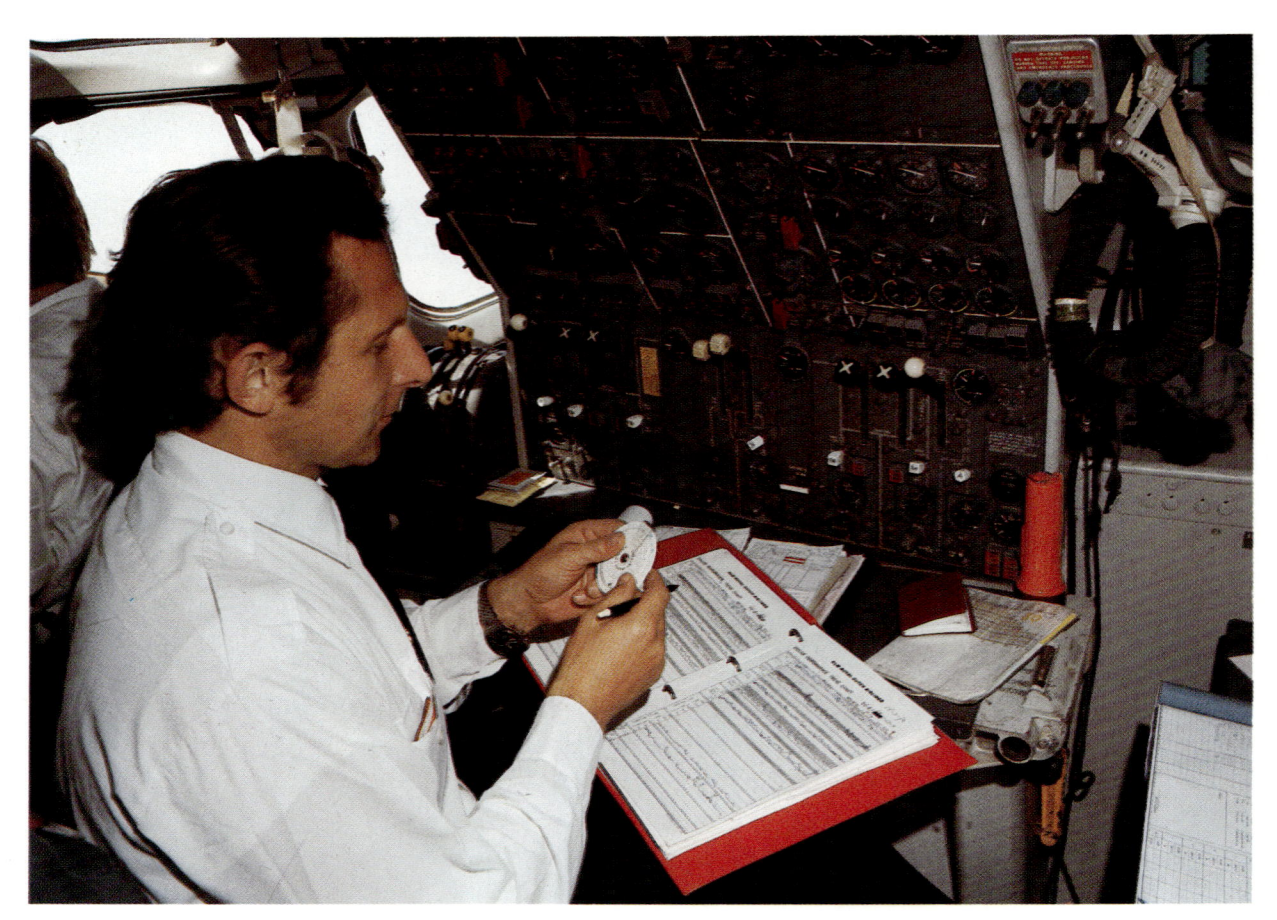

Airliners burn up huge amounts of **aviation fuel**. Some use as much as 8000 litres an hour. This is why the fuel tanks of a jumbo jet are designed to hold 100 000 litres of fuel. The equivalent amount of petrol would keep a family car going for 100 years!

Refuelling

Many workers are employed to bring fuel to the planes as they stand on the apron outside the terminal. The tanker drivers know that a plane must be filled up quickly between flights to prevent delay to passengers or cargo. They refill the tanks with aviation fuel. Each driver can bring between 20 000 and 40 000 litres of fuel to the plane in a single tanker. High-speed pumps push the fuel through fuel lines into the plane. Even so, it may take up to 20 minutes to fill up the tanks of a jumbo jet.

How much fuel?

Huge quantities of fuel are very heavy for a plane to carry. A jumbo jet may be carrying over 50 tonnes of fuel at take-off.

Taking on fuel

Extra weight slows down the plane and may mean that fewer passengers can be carried. This is why the captain of a plane has to work out exactly how much fuel the plane will need on the journey. It will depend partly on the speed of the plane and its weight including passengers, cargo and fuel. It will also depend on the strength of the winds and the direction from which they are blowing.

Weather forecasts inform the captain of the winds the plane will face on the journey. If the winds are blowing from behind the plane, it will use less fuel. If they are in front, the plane will use more. When the captain has worked out how much fuel is needed, he or she gives this information to the tanker drivers. They fill up the plane's tanks with that amount, together with a small amount in reserve in case of an emergency.

Storing fuel

After filling up a plane, the airport tanker drivers collect more fuel from the fuel depot on the edge of the airport. At some airports, however, the fuel is piped underground directly from the depot to the apron outside the terminal. From there it can then be pumped directly into the airliner's fuel tanks. This method is safe and lessens the fire risk.

▶ Aviation fuel is carried in tankers from the main depot, or storage area, to the plane waiting on the apron. The fuel is then pumped on board the aircraft.

The flight crew

While the passengers are checking in, the flight crew of the airliner prepare for take-off. The captain and the first officer study the **flight plan**. This is the timetable showing the route to be taken by the plane, its speed, the height at which it will fly, and the time it is expected to arrive. The plan is prepared by the captain with the help of experts in the airline's **operations and control room**.

Before the flight, the members of the flight crew look at the weather reports. They are also told how many passengers and how much cargo the plane will be carrying.

Flying the plane

First the crew go on board and make a **pre-flight check** to see that all the instruments are working properly. The instruments give the flight crew the information that they need to fly the plane. They show how high the plane is flying, its speed, direction, how much fuel is left and whether the engines are working properly.

The captain sits in the left-hand seat in front of the controls on the **flight deck**. The first officer, or **co-pilot**, sits in front of a second set of controls on the right. On large airliners, there is usually an engineering officer who sits behind the captain and gives technical support. The captain is in complete charge of the airliner. There may be as many as 500 passengers on board, and a jumbo jet is worth a great deal of money. It is important that great care is taken.

◀ The captain being briefed on the type of weather he will meet during the flight. High winds will affect the amount of fuel the plane needs to carry.

The flight crew

A skilled job

Flying an airliner is a highly skilled job. Some airline pilots first learn to fly in the air force. Others join the airline straight from college. All pilots have to be healthy and fit, and they must have regular medical check-ups.

Even when pilots have qualified, they have to continue their training because they must be prepared for anything that may happen. To do this, they use a **flight simulator**. This is a machine which looks like the real flight deck of an airliner. Each time the pilot touches the controls of the simulator, a computer is programmed to make the machine move like an airliner. It is possible to imitate bad weather and emergency situations, such as engine failure or overshooting the runway. Pilots can train like this without the risk of an actual accident.

▲ The flight deck of an airliner is full of instruments. This vast array of dials, knobs and switches enables the flight crew to fly the airliner to its destination in safety. Everything must be checked before take-off.

▼ Most pilots learn how to fly a new type of plane by sitting at the controls of a flight simulator like this one.

On the plane

When passengers board a plane they are greeted by the members of the cabin crew. These are the flight attendants, the pursers, stewards and stewardesses whose job it is to look after the passengers during the flight. The flight attendants show the passengers to their seats, answer their questions and try to solve any problems the passengers may have. They also have to make sure that all the passengers' hand luggage is safely put away under the seat or in overhead lockers.

Safety first

Safety is an important part of the attendants' duties. The attendants check that all passengers put on their safety belts before take-off and landing. They demonstrate how to put on **lifejackets** and point out the emergency exits. All the members of the cabin crew are trained to operate and use the emergency chutes. These are special tubes or slides that the passengers and crew can use to escape from the plane after an accident.

The crew are all fully trained to cope with anything that may happen. They know how to fight a fire if it breaks out on board the plane while it is in flight. They are also trained in **first aid** in case of accident or illness during the flight.

◀ The stewards and stewardesses tell the passengers what to do in case of emergency. At the start of the flight, they show the passengers how to operate lifejackets and how to use oxygen masks.

On the plane

▲ It is the job of the cabin crew to see that passengers have a comfortable flight. They may have to reassure first-time travellers or look after small children. Here, the stewardesses are preparing drinks in the galley, or kitchen, of the airliner.

▼ Passengers on most flights are given something to eat and drink on board.

Serving food

The members of the cabin crew also serve meals and drinks to the passengers. They do not cook the food on the plane. Instead the meals are cooked and prepared in advance. Trucks take the food to the plane just before it leaves. The food is heated in the galley of the plane in a microwave oven during the flight.

To help in their training, the cabin crew learn their duties on the ground in a full-size model of a passenger cabin.

A rewarding job

Working as a member of the cabin crew is a hard but interesting job. Crew members work long hours, but many of them travel all over the world. They may be away from home for several days at a time if they are on an international flight. Many members of the cabin crew are appointed because they can speak more than one language.

Take-off!

All the fuel needed for the flight is on board, the baggage and cargo are loaded, and the meals for the flight are in the galley. All the service vehicles that have been loading these items onto the plane have moved away from the airliner. The cabin crew count the passengers to make sure that the numbers agree with those on the check-in list.

Shortly before take-off a powerful tractor, called an **air tug**, pulls the airliner away from the pier or terminal. Inside the cabin, smokers must put out their cigarettes and all passengers must fasten their seat belts. The cabin crew make sure this is done.

▼ An air tug tows a Boeing 747 into position so that the pilot can use the airliner's engines to taxi onto the runway.

Final checks

The members of the flight crew make their final check. When they are ready, they radio the control tower. They ask permission to start the engines. When this is given, engineers on the apron start the engines with a power source on wheels, known as a **mobile generator**.

The pilot moves the plane slowly down the taxiway leading to the end of the runway. There, the plane has to wait before the ground control gives it permission to take off. There is a short pause while the flight crew check their engines and instruments for the last time before take-off. The control tower then gives the go-ahead, and the engines are switched on to full power.

The flight crew release the airliner's brakes. The plane starts to move. It goes faster and faster. It may cover a distance of over three kilometres before it is travelling fast enough to leave the ground. The pilot touches the controls and the wings lift the plane off the runway, and it climbs steeply into the sky.

Take-off!

▲ The minute the plane leaves the runway, the pilot puts it into a steep climb in order to avoid any tall buildings, and to cause the least noise disturbance to people living near the airport.

The flight

During the flight the members of the crew keep in touch with the ground by radio. Once the course of the flight has been set, they can leave the plane in the hands of the **automatic pilot**. This is the machine which automatically alters the direction of the airliner so that it will stay on course without assistance from the pilot. The flight crew keep in touch with the air traffic controllers in charge of the airspace through which they are travelling. English is used throughout the world as the language of the controllers.

When the airliner is close to its destination, the flight crew radio approach control in the airport control tower. They are given permission to land, and a radar operator guides them as they land.

▲ From the moment that a plane approaches an airport until the moment that the plane lands, the pilot is in constant radio contact with air traffic control.

Flying cargo

Most airports do a lot of business with firms which send cargo by air instead of by rail, sea or road. About half the world's air cargo travels in the hold of passenger airliners. The other half travels in special cargo planes which have their own terminal at an airport.

The cargo terminal is usually situated on the edge of the airport. It can easily be reached by truck drivers bringing cargo to the terminal on the roads leading to the airport.

Sorting cargo

The cargo is stored in warehouses at the cargo terminal before and after a flight. The cargo terminal workers label the cargo and use computers to calculate the cost of transport. They also calculate how much cargo can be loaded into each plane.

The goods are then sorted for the different flights. They have to be checked against the list of goods travelling on a particular flight. All cargo is also checked by the customs officers. Some goods are packed into large metal containers called 'igloos'. These boxes have been specially shaped to fit neatly into the space inside the body of the airliner. Other goods are placed on flat trays usually made of wood.

▼ When animals, whether giraffes or chickens, are sent by air, the greatest care should be taken to ensure that they travel safely. The advantage of sending animals by air is that they will arrive at their destination much quicker than by sea or land.

Flying cargo

▶ Cargo handlers use a special machine to lift cargo on a platform until it is level with the floor of the hold of the airliner. The handlers then load the cargo into the hold so that the weight is spread evenly.

Why use a plane?

Sending cargo by plane is costly. It is only worthwhile if the goods are likely to spoil quickly, like fresh flowers, or if they have a high value. Goods are also sent by air if they are needed urgently, such as letters, medical supplies, newspapers and vital parts for engines or machines.

Some types of cargo have to be guarded by security officers. Valuable cargo like this may include large amounts of money, precious stones, costly jewellery and even gold bars.

Loading cargo

The cargo handlers have to move cargo of all shapes and sizes. There can be anything from live monkeys and fresh fruit to cars and furniture. In larger airports, the cargo handlers use forklift trucks, small cranes or conveyor belts to move goods into the cargo hold of the plane. Engineers open the tail or the nose of the plane to make it easier to load. The cargo hold of a plane is fitted with rails and rollers. These are used to slide the containers and trays into the hold of the plane.

The future

No one knows what it will be like to work at an airport in the future. It is possible that huge jumbo jets flying faster than Concorde may carry thousands of passengers in one plane from Sydney to New York or London. If this happened, then air travel would be very much cheaper than it is at present.

Fuel

Such flights would only be possible if a better and cheaper fuel for aircraft engines was found. Some people fear that airports will in fact be closed down because the world's supplies of oil will run out. It is possible to make aviation fuel from coal but at the moment this costs too much.

▼ Airports of the future could be very different from airports today. Many things will have changed and the jobs people do will be different too.

The future

▲ Some people think the airports of the future will be seadromes. They could be built on long platforms reaching out into the sea. Airports like this would have many advantages. There would be no hills or buildings to get in the way when airliners landed. Only a very few people would be bothered by the noise.

Short and long runways

Planes of the future may need much less fuel than at present. They may need shorter runways as well. If this happened, then the need for large airports would no longer exist. Small airliners could take off from the roofs of buildings in the city centres just like helicopters do today.

However, if airliners were designed to travel faster, they would need very long runways. If this were to happen, the airports would have to be moved farther away from the cities. They could be built over the sea where there is plenty of space.

New airports

Whatever happens, it is likely that the airports of the future will be run more and more by computers and automatic machines. These could do many of the jobs done by people at present. Automatic ticket machines might take the place of the staff at the check-in desk. Computers could be programmed to answer passenger's questions in any language. Automatic machines would serve hot food and drinks, and there might even be automatic security checks. Even the airliners could be staffed by robots and automatic pilots. Whatever the future brings, airports will always be exciting and busy places to work.

Glossary

administrator: a person who is in charge of the running of a big organization such as an airport

airline: a company which provides flights from place to place

airliner: a large aircraft owned by an airline which carries passengers and cargo

airmail: letters or parcels which are carried by plane

airport authority: the organization which runs an airport

airspace: the area of sky above a particular country

air traffic controller: an official, usually based at an airport, who controls the movement of aircraft in the air or on the ground

air tug: a powerful vehicle used to pull or push airliners into position on the ground at an airport

airworthy: describes a plane which is safe to fly

approach control: the group of people who are in charge of plane movements near an airport

apron: the area of concrete or tarmac outside an airport terminal which is used by planes

automatic pilot: a machine or process which keeps an aircraft flying on a fixed course on its own

aviation fuel: the type of fuel which is burned by an aircraft's engines

baggage train: a long line of wagons which carry baggage

boarding pass: a card issued to a passenger enabling him or her to board an aircraft

cargo: the goods carried by a ship or plane

cargo hold: the space in a ship or on an aircraft used for carrying goods

carousel: a roundabout. Baggage is put on a carousel in an airport for passengers to claim their luggage after a flight

check in: to report at an airport with a ticket and baggage before a flight

chemical foam: a mixture of froth and bubbles produced by chemicals. It smothers flames and prevents air getting to them

control tower: the tall building at an airport where all the orders are given to planes at or near the airport

conveyor belt: a continuous moving track which is used to carry goods from one place to another

co-pilot: the pilot who assists the captain of an aircraft

customs: the place where goods or baggage are checked by government officers. These officers make sure that the correct taxes are paid on goods entering or leaving the country. They also check that no forbidden goods or animals are being carried. Customs officers also check passengers' passports

domestic flight: a flight which takes place entirely inside a country

duty free: describes goods on which no tax has been charged

first aid: immediate help given to someone who is ill or injured

flight deck: the place from which the pilot and other members of the flight crew operate the airliner

flight plan: the details of the route to be taken by an aircraft and how long the flight will take

flight simulator: a machine which imitates the movements of an airliner in flight. It is used to train pilots and flight engineers

fuel depot: a storage place for fuel

gate: the door through which passengers leave the terminal building in order to board a plane

ground controller: the person in the airport control tower who controls the movements of aircraft on the ground

hangar: a large building where planes are kept or are taken to be repaired. Cargo is also stored in a hangar

health control: the group of officials who enforce government orders concerning public health

immigration control: a government department which controls the entry of people into a country

jumbo jet: a huge airliner. The phrase is most often used to describe the Boeing 747 airliner

lifejacket: a type of sleeveless jacket which fills up with air and keeps a person's head above water in order to prevent drowning

metal detector: a machine or device which can find objects made of metal in a passenger's clothes or baggage

mobile generator: an electric generator mounted on a vehicle. It is used at an airport to make enough electricity to start the engines of an airliner

operations and control room: the room from which an airline organizes the movements of its airliners around the world

overhaul: to give an engine, machine, or vehicle a thorough check-up and service

Glossary

passport: a small book given to someone by a country's government to say that he or she is from that country and may travel abroad

pier: a long building at an airport leading from the terminal building to the waiting airliners

pre-flight check: the check made by the members of the flight crew of an airliner before take-off

protective clothing: clothes which protect people, such as fire officers, against dangerous conditions

quarantine: the place where, or the period of time when, people or animals are kept apart from each other in order to stop the spread of a disease

radar: a method of using radio beams to detect the position of objects in the distance, such as aircraft

security officer: an official employed at an airport to ensure the safety of the airport workers and passengers

shuttle flight: a regular air service used by passengers who do not need to book a ticket in advance

smuggle: to secretly carry something, such as illegal drugs, into another country

stack: a line of aircraft at an airport waiting to land. Planes stack by flying around at different heights above and below each other

taxiway: a wide concrete pathway which connects the runway and the apron

terminal: a building at an airport where passengers or cargo arrive at or depart from

transponder: an electronic device fitted to an airliner which allows details of the flight to be picked up by radar

visa: a document which gives a person permission to enter a foreign country for a specific purpose or period of time

visual inspection: a careful physical check made by someone without the aid of instruments or machines

X-ray machine: a device used at airports to check the contents of passengers' baggage

Index

accident 11, 28, 29
administrator 10
air traffic control 5, 30, 31, 40, 41
air tug 40
airline 4
airliner 4
airmail 7, 43
airport authority 10
airport manager 10, 11
airspace 9
airworthy 32
Alcock, John 6
animals 23
approach control 31
apron 19, 25
Atlantic Ocean 6
automatic pilot 41
aviation fuel 34

baggage
  check-in 16, 17
  customs check 22
  handling 18, 19
  security check 20, 21
baggage handler 18, 19
baggage train 19
birds 27
Bleriot, Louis 6
boarding pass 17, 24
breathing apparatus 29

captain 36
car parking 14
cargo hold 18, 42, 43
carousel 19
check-in desk 16, 17
chemical foam 29
Chicago 8
cleaners 15
code 18, 30
computer
  air traffic control 30
  airport automation 45
  check-in 17
  cost calculations 42
  flight display 24
  flight simulator 37
  passport check 22
  security 20
control tower 5
  air traffic 30, 31
  taxiway 25

conveyor belt 17, 18, 43
co-pilot 36
customs 22, 23
  cargo check 42

departure lounge 24
disease 23
domestic flight 5
  shuttle 16
drugs 22
duty free 13

electrical engineer 27
electrician 15
emergency 11, 28, 29
emergency chute 38
engineer
  checking aircraft 25, 32, 33
  runway design 26
engineering officer 36
England 6, 7
explosive 20

fire service 11, 28, 29
first aid 38
first airports 6, 7
first officer 36
flight attendants 38, 39
flight crew 36, 37
flight deck 36, 37
flight number 18, 30
flight plan 36
flight simulator 37
fork-lift truck 43
France 6, 7
fuel 34, 35, 44
fuel depot 25, 35
fuel tanker 25, 34

galley 39
ground controller 30
guns 20, 21

hand baggage 17, 38
hangar 33
health control 23
Hong Kong 9

illness 23, 38
immigration control 22, 23
infectious disease 23
internal flight 5, 8, 16

jet engine 7
jumbo jet 7

King Khalid International Airport 8
Kitty Hawk 6

landing light 27
Lhasa 8
life jacket 38

manager 10, 11
maintenance
  aircraft 32
  airport 27
medical services 11, 15
metal detector 21
microwave oven 39
mobile generator 40

noise 9

O'Hare International Airport 8
operations and control room 36
overhaul 33

passenger cabin 38, 39
passport 22
  customs check 13
perishable goods 43
pilot 36, 37
plumber 15
police service 11, 15
  emergency 28
  security 20
pre-flight check 36
protective clothing 29
purser 38

quarantine 23

radar 30
radio contact 30
rescue 28, 29
restaurant 15
Riyadh 8
robot 45
runway 4, 26, 27
  at first airports 7
  length of 45
  traffic control 30

safety
  accidents 29
  international 9
  on the plane 38
safety belt 38
Saudi Arabia 8
seat belt 38

security officer 20, 21
  cargo protection 43
servicing aircraft 32
shop assistant 15
shuttle flight 16
site for airport 9
smuggling 22, 23
sniffer dog 22
snow clearing 27
sorting room 18
stack 31
steward 38, 39
stewardess 38, 39

take-off 40, 41
tanker 25, 34
taxiway 25, 30
terminal 11, 12, 13, 14, 15
Tibet 8
ticket 16, 17
Tonga 8
transponder 30
transport workers 14

United States 6
  busiest airport 8
  import controls 23

visa 22

waiter 15
waitress 15
weapons 20, 21
weather 35
Wright, Orville 6
Wright, Wilbur 6

X-ray machine
  security 21
  plane overhaul 33